OTIS Otis College of Art and Design

BEN MALTZ GALLERY

ALISON SAAR

STILL...

CONTENTS

Introduction by Meg Linton 7

Spirits in My Head by Harryette Mullen 10

Still Defined by Barbara Thompson, Ph. D. 13

Anatomy by Harryette Mullen 21

Work 22

Shedding Skin by Harryette Mullen 39

Exhibition Checklist 40

Exhibition Tour 41

Artist Biography 43

Acknowledgements 45

Otis College of Art and Design 46

Previous:
Rouse, 2012 (detail)
Wood, bronze, paper and
antler sheds
90 x 76 x 73 inches

Left:
Installation View, 2012
Ben Maltz Gallery
Otis College of Art and Design

ALISON SAAR: STILL

Informed by artistic traditions from the Americas to Africa and beyond, and by her mixed racial upbringing, Alison Saar fuses her paradoxical responses to the black-and-white delineations of political and social forces into a powerful, visual, and kinesthetic tension. She uses the history and associations of her materials, everyday experience, African art and ritual, Greek mythology, and the stark sculptural tradition of German Expressionism to infuse her work with a primal intensity that challenges cultural and historic references and stereotypes.

The metaphorical armature supporting, entwining, embracing this selection of new sculpture is the myriad of meanings for the word "still." Saar teases out the complexities of this little noun/verb in bold and subtle ways. Four stylized glass "stills" express the personal and political challenges of being an artist, woman, and mother in the twenty-first century. These interactive idiosyncratic stills attempt to distill the vile essence of bigotry and transform it into consciousness. Only through awareness and informed mindfulness can negative representations be dispelled and converted into positive reflections.

In contrast to the rustic, mechanical, fragmented feel of the stills, are Saar's figures. These various hybrid creatures stem from trees or boast antlers. They stand at the threshold, caught or balancing between free will and innate evolution. They are mythical portends of inevitable change—shedding fertility to reveal the next saga. For example, *Rouse* (2012) depicts a strong, dark, compact woman with a semi-transparent embryonic shell of a female figure nestled and bound inside her large antlers. Saar's inspiration for this work was watching her daughter grow from a teenager to an adult. It also mirrors her desire to remake herself, to emerge from one state of creative pursuit and production to another.

Saar, an alumna from Otis' Graduate Fine Arts program in 1981, is a mature and significant sculptor who has achieved broad recognition for her studio and public art throughout the country. Her work is held in many collections including the Museum of Modern Art, Hirshhorn Museum and Sculpture Garden, and Metropolitan Museum of Art; and she has major public art works in Los Angeles, New York, and Chicago. She has received numerous prestigious awards from the Guggenheim Foundation, Anonymous Was a Woman, and the National Endowment for the Arts.

The Ben Maltz Gallery is dedicated to providing a space, and an encouraging atmosphere, for artists to experiment with materials and ideas outside their usual practice. It has been a pleasure and an honor to work with Alison Saar over the last two years and watch her struggle and thrive to bring this challenging body of work into being. As with every exhibition of this caliber there are dozens of people working behind the scenes who make it all possible and we have acknowledged their efforts separately in this publication.

Rouse, 2012
Wood, bronze, paper and
antler sheds
90 x 76 x 73 inches

We also recognize the generous support of the Contemporary Collectors – Orange County who have funded this publication which includes a thoughtful essay by Barbara Thompson entitled "Still Defined" and three poems by noted poet Harryette Mullen. Lastly, we want to thank Sunny War for bringing her music to this project and Rebecca Walker for joining us to share in a dynamic conversation with the artist and Otis community as part of our public programming.

Saar's work echoes an entirely American process of spiritual and political bifurcation, and the evolution of historical recovery. As Lowry Stokes Sims, Curator at the Museum of Arts and Design, wrote, "Alison Saar's library of references is as varied and rich as her own heritage. Her special gift lies in her ability to translate the personal and the culturally specific in such a way that it embodies concerns that not only transcend race but also gender."*

Meg Linton
Director of Galleries and Exhibitions
Curator of the Exhibition
Otis Ben Maltz Gallery

Installation View, 2012
Ben Maltz Gallery
Otis College of Art and Design

*Lowry Stokes Sims, "Alison Saar's Feallan and Fallow: Seasons, Colors, Race and Gender," in *Feallan and Fallow: Alison Saar.* New York: Mad. Sq. Art, 2011, p. 43.

SPIRITS IN MY HEAD

Spirits in my head,
drunk on moonshine,
intoxicated by white lightning,
tipsy with joy juice.

Spirits in my head,
caught in the wind,
rinsed in the rain,
dried in the sun.

Spirits in my head,
springing to life like dandelions,
tangled as a briar patch,
wild as African orchids.

Harryette Mullen

STILL DEFINED

In the English language, "still" is a wonderfully complex and poetic word that covers a wide range of ideas, actions, and descriptions. In her new solo exhibition, *STILL...*, Alison Saar beautifully captures and plays with the subtle elasticity of meanings and uses of "still." Saar's witty titles and visual punning reveal her continued fascination with lexis and metaphor, while concealing darker issues of oppression, poverty, and human devaluation that lie just under the surface of American society.

---

still:
silence; tranquility; a distilling apparatus; appease; dispel; banish; cause to subside; immobile; subdued; obsolete; dead at birth; continuing now or in the future as in the past; yet; nonetheless; in spite of everything; static; stagnant...

Rendered in Saar's signature style, the new work features crudely constructed armatures, apparatus, and mechanics made from copper, lead, steel, rusty chains, and rope that interact with a cast of life-size characters. Roughly soldered copper pipes connect to clear rubber tubing running through, into, and out of figurative glass vessels. These hollow and transparent vessels contain red, black, and murky liquids, which the viewer can activate by squeezing simple black pumps. Saar's mechanics and her use of copper pipes and coiled tubing quickly bring to mind a by-gone era of the Temperance Movement, Prohibition, and Great Depression when alcohol manufacture, distribution, and sales were banned, leading to the illegal brewing of hard liquors in backyard stills. [i]

In 2011, Saar was invited as an artist-in-residence at Pilchuk Glass School, thus opening up new ways of thinking about her practice and allowing her to combine more familiar materials, such as wood, bronze, and found objects with glass, a medium she has never worked with before. "I went there thinking 'I don't know what I'm going to do' but I was really interested in glassware from labs... and experimenting.... From there it went into this weird stage between laboratory, science experiments, and stills."[ii] Saar became particularly interested in the aesthetics of hand-made, backyard stills, "the moonshine ones, funky burn marks, and soldering." The "stills" that began at Pilchuck as ideas, now fully rigged, are metaphors of the commoditized human body—valuable if functional, obsolete if not.

Previous:
50 Proof, 2012 (detail)
Glass, copper, rubber
steel, soap, cotton
textiles, enamel basin
and water
63 x 27 x 20 inches

Left:
Still Run Dry, 2012 (detail)
Glass, copper, rubber,
lead and steel
75 x 116 x 14 inches

As the title implies, *Still Run Dry* no longer produces precious, vital, or intoxicating liquids. It has no mechanics; its hollow parts—a heart, lungs, stomach, intestines, breasts, uterus, and ovaries—do not function. The clear glass organs, placed on shelves are "like specimens... lab-like." These body parts seem to have once contained liquids but are now dried up, dirty, and caked with dust. "Super derelict," as Saar notes.

The armature of the dysfunctional still complements the empty organs and includes blown and burnt out copper piping and torn rubber tubing that resembles "an experiment gone awry or neglected." More directly, though, *Still Run Dry* deals with sexism and ageism in which "women [are] valued by the functioning body. When their bodies stop functioning then they are [rendered] derelict and put up on the shelf." Saar's banishment of a woman's body parts to a shelf emphasizes the cultural devaluation of women as scientific specimens. The presence of defunct burners endows the installation with an even more distressing sense of the laboratory where clandestine experiments occur, which Saar enhances by reversing the order of a uterus containing a pomegranate feeding coal-filled ovaries. Now in her mid-fifties, Saar presents the quiet dismay of barrenness, of fertility run dry, while voicing a sharp critique of the commoditization of woman as a life-giving machine and subsequent devaluation when this role ends.

Dis·till:
Condense; cleansing; purify; sanitize; decontaminate; refine; concentrate; abbreviate; reduce; summarize; abridge; extract; glean; cull; collect; gather; remove; extort...

Saar is known for highly personalized art that addresses her struggles with the contradictions between an outwardly Caucasian appearance and personal identification with her mother's African American heritage. In the new sculpture *50 Proof*, Saar tackles the painful realities of being "half-black, half-white" through a rendition of "the tragic mulatto" stereotype, who seems to be undergoing a kind of cleansing or purification through the mechanism of a still. In her usual fashion, Saar's sharp wit in titling this piece poetically plays with the unit of measurement for alcohol content in liquor. Ironically, in the context of backyard stills, 50 proof would be considered an extraordinarily weak distillation of moonshine, which is usually about 190 proof or 95% alcohol.

Frederick Merchant,
Blockade Stills, c. 1917,
Durwood Barbour Collection
of North Carolina Postcards,
North Carolina Collection
Photographic Archives,
Wilson Library, University of
North Carolina at Chapel Hill

50 Proof is composed of a female head and heart made of clear glass. Ink feeds from the heart into the lower half of the head. When activated by the squeeze pump, a slow trickle spills out of the woman's eyes, her black tears splattering into a white washbasin and indelibly staining two white hand towels hanging from racks. Coal Tar and Ivory soap placed on a shelf offer up a metaphoric cleansing: a choice between black and white. The irony of this soap selection is especially germane. Ivory soap is popularly known in America for its catchy advertising of being so pure that it floats. Coal Tar soap, on the other hand, has a more ambiguous nature. Derived from a liquid byproduct of distilled coal, tar soap is an antiseptic that draws out toxins from the body and has therefore been used or prescribed as a cleanser for a variety of skin disorders. However, it can also irritate or redden the skin, cause increased sun sensitivity, and is cancerous. Hence, it has both purifying and contaminating properties.[iii]

50 Proof evokes a turn-of-the-century domestic setting. Rigged to the still, the vintage washstand has an eerie overtone of an old hospital lab. The copper tubing, with its varied dark blue, black, and brown patina, contributes a sense of experimentation while implying also the passage of time and history. The metal armature around the woman's neck, which holds the glass head in place, reinforces the notion of history, recalling images of slave chain gangs, their necks, hands, and feet in iron shackles. The black tears running down the face into the basin—like indelible words and splotches of ink on paper—seem to be spilling over this sordid episode of human history.

Mammy Machine and *Black Lightning* riff off "stills" and "distillation" to signify the reduction or essentialization of humans into stereotypes. *Mammy Machine* includes a vintage washbasin and a copper armature holding a cluster of nine glass bottles in various breast shapes and shades of brown. Squeezing the rubber pump causes this literal "milking machine" to stream water out from the nipples.

The "still" clearly references stereotypes of women of color as washerwomen, mammies, and wet nurses, who take care of other peoples' children while leaving their own behind. As Saar points out, such stereotypes exist today. "Society still perpetuates them…a person of color is often paid a fraction of the salary as a white nanny." Society values the mammy, her milk, and labor as commodities, thus demeaning the person. This makes the milk, Saar asserts, "like dirty dish water."

While *Mammy Machine* draws attention to economic oppression of women of color and subsequent consequences of poverty in America today, racism is also at the core of *Black Lightning*. The title of *Black Lightning* places a racial twist on an alternate name for moonshine, also called white lightning, mountain dew, mother's milk, hooch, stump water, and Tennessee white whiskey. This illegal clear liquid was historically distilled from corn into a very high proof spirit using small-scale, homemade backyard stills usually made of copper. Although "white lightning" is popularly associated with the Appalachian hills and Prohibition, it has a long history in America spanning back to the Revolutionary and U.S. Civil Wars, when the government taxed liquors to pay for war. Impoverished by the declined value of corn as food produce, many farmers turned to the illegal distillation and distribution of this potent yet highly commoditized liquor.[iv]

Saar's "still," *Black Lightning*, is comprised of a pair of boxing gloves hanging from the wall and a mop and bucket. Red fluid pumps from the bucket through copper tubing into the clear glass boxing gloves, which when filled with the red liquid begins to trickle out of holes in the wrists. Saar created this sculpture as a critique of the inequitable and stereotypical labor options attributed or open to black men. While the visual reference to boxing as suicide becomes particularly poignant in a contemporary context in relation to the high rate of violent death among African American male youths today, this sculpture also points to "the still prevalent view that if you're an African American male you can either be a super star, like Michael Jackson, or a janitor. You can't be President. Even though we have a black president, people don't believe it, still!"

Saar's personal struggle with her own mixed heritage makes her especially aware of the racial politics associated with President Obama's bi-racial identity. She is particularly troubled that both the European American and African American communities deny him kinship. "Whites say, no, he's not white. Blacks say, no, he's not black enough....All of this stuff is now coming to the surface [because] racism is still deeply, deeply ingrained in American society." *Black Lightning* thus subtly expresses the artist's rage over the persistent and blatant expressions of racism in American politics and public commentary, which seem to be reverting to a time when racial slurs were an acceptable norm. "That's what got my blood boiling. It's got me simmerin', so to speak." As a nation, we remain still... continuing now or in the future as in the past.

---

weight:
measure of heaviness; object used to exert a force; standard of comparison; object used to hold
something else down; counterbalance; heavy object; corpulence; oppressiveness; burden of responsibilities;
preponderance; importance...

Saar carefully selects found objects imbued with the marks of their former lives and histories and often incorporates them into her work. For example, *Weight* features a young black girl on a swing dangling from a cotton scale. She is counterbalanced by a coalscuttle, its contents spilling out toward the ground: an iron ladle, horseshoe, sickle, lock and key, shackle, pair of scissors, potato masher, shovel, hot comb for the hair, rope, boxing gloves, skillets, flat irons, and chains. "I started thinking of it as a kind of cornucopia," Saar explains, "about [the girl's] opportunities, and what her value is... as a slave or as a domestic. She can be a hairdresser. She can work in the field. She can be a seamstress, a cook.... but," Saar pauses to point to the tattered pair of boxing gloves, "she has to fight her way out."

Theoretically, a cornucopia symbolizes wealth, harvest, and good fortune. But Saar's version relates to cotton wealth, made possible by the exploitation and dehumanization of slaves. And although the image of a young black girl on a swing commonly alludes to youth, innocence, and hope, this child is precariously balanced by a "cornucopia of troubles and turmoil." The removal of a single object from the coalscuttle will send her crashing to the ground. More importantly, the young girl is covered in coal dust, naked, and swinging on ropes made sticky with smears of tar. The swing hangs from a tree root jarringly reminiscent of the lynching of African Americans and the weighing of slaves sold at market by the pound.

---

un·done:
not done; accomplished or completed; unfinished; unfastened; untied; brought to destruction;
ruin or disaster; destroyed; erased or effaced...

In *Undone*, a black female figure levitates overhead, sitting on a chair hung from the wall. A translucent white gown, clutched in her hands, cascades about 16 feet to the ground, the edge stained red as though soiled by blood from an umbilicus-like cord dangling down between her legs. Made from tree branches, the cord has an arterial, unfinished, and almost abortive feel. The mature woman in *Undone* is ghost-like, suggesting funerary shrouds and death, which in many cultures represent not the end of life but rebirth into the realm of ancestral spirits that guide humans through difficult and challenging times.

Like the murky residue left inside old glass bottles tied to the umbilical cord, this sculpture relates to the fermentation not of potent liquors but of new ideas, "some unformed, others not followed through." This woman, though undone, is an extension of Saar herself, gravitating toward a transformational moment when the old begins to fade and the new comes to fruition.

---

rouse:
awaken from unconsciousness; activate; energize; stimulate; incite; instigate;
provoke someone's anger or action; hunt; force; or drive out; displace or chase away; turn back...

Saar finds herself, as a mature artist and mother of young adults, in a metamorphic state, still undefined but "approaching completion." She beautifully captures this notion in *Rouse,* a life-sized sculpture of a light-skinned woman, attached like an embryo to a massive nest of antlers growing from the head of a sturdy graphite-colored figure. The reclining and hollow figure is molded from rice paper and glue, thus reinforcing her fragile nature. Despite her visceral and incomplete form, like Saar, she is coming out of a state of hibernation, arousing from "the incubation of ideas to a new self, the pupa stage of insects, or the shedding of old skin and the formation of the new." Saar explains that *Rouse* is about her daughter Maddy leaving for college and the fragile nature of her emergence into the adult world.

In stark contrast to the fetal figure, the standing figure—representing Saar's own primal animal-self, the fierce mother trying to protect her offspring—is made from a patchwork of unrefined blocks of carved wood. Her spent antlers litter the ground as symbols of protection, maturity, and the passage of time. Not yet derelict, she is nonetheless beginning to show "the fissures of a body in decline... preparing for and holding it together long enough for the next one to take over... to come to term." Speaking from a stream of consciousness, Saar expounds that *Rouse*, like the other works in this exhibition, is "about me being menopausal, being interested in moving into new territory in my work, having new ideas, new materials, and that I don't know what any of it is, and that I'm doing things on precipices, ready to cut away the old self but trying to find the stillness to let this other part of me mature and come out and be realized."

In all their diversity and weight as visual, lexical, and historical allusions to racism, ageism, and sexism, the new works in *STILL...* clearly declare the core notion that Saar finds herself in a particularly fragile moment. She is roused from a state of incubation, energized with new ideas that have yet to take full form. Saar's renewed engagement with herself is taking her art beyond her current place as a mother facing the empty nest. "Even though I've had a career all this time, I'm still extremely dedicated to getting [my children] to school or picking them up and all that." Almost speaking in a whisper, she continues, "It's going to really change. I feel like I have to... let go of control... and remake myself."

Saar becomes very still...

Barbara Thompson, Ph.D.
Phyllis Wattis Curator of the Arts of Africa and the Americas
Cantor Arts Center, Stanford University

Barbara Thompson received her Ph.D. in art history from the University of Iowa. She is now the Curator of the Arts of Africa and the Americas at the Cantor Arts Center, Stanford University before which she was Curator of African, Oceanic, and Native American Collections at the Hood Museum of Art, Dartmouth College. She has taught art history and anthropology at the University of Iowa and the University of Northern Iowa. She specializes in historical arts from east Africa as well as in contemporary arts from Africa and the Diaspora. Her exhibitions and scholarly publications include projects such as *Crossing Currents: The Synergy of Jean Michel Basquiat and Ouattara Watts* (2003); *A Point of View: Africa on Display?* (2003–4); *So Much Trouble in The World—Believe It or Not!, a site-specific installation by Fred Wilson* (2005), and *Black Womanhood: Images, Icons, and Ideologies of the African Body* (2008).

END NOTES:

i. For historical interpretations of alcohol reform in the U.S., see Eric Burns, 2004, *The Spirits of America: A Social History of Alcohol*, Philadelphia, Pa: Temple University Press; John Kobler, 1973, *Ardent Spirits: The Rise and Fall of Prohibition*, New York: Putnam; and John J. Rumbarger, 1989, *Profits, Power, and Prohibition: Alcohol Reform and the Industrializing of America*, 1800-1930, Albany: State University of New York Press.

ii. This and all subsequent quotes are derived from an interview conducted by the author with Alison Saar at her studio in Los Angeles on July 28, 2012.

iii. Philip Ross, "Occupational Skin Lesions Due To Pitch And Tar," *The British Medical Journal*, Vol. 2, No. 4572 (Aug. 21, 1948), pp. 369-374.

iv. Bruce E. Stewart, "Attacking 'Red-Legged Grasshoppers': Moonshiners, Violence, and the Politics of Federal Liquor Taxation in Western North Carolina, 1865-1876," *Appalachian Journal*, Vol. 32, No. 1 (FALL 2004), pp. 26-48 and Loyal Durand, Jr., "'Mountain Moonshining' in East Tennessee," Geographical Review, Vol. 46, No. 2 (Apr., 1956), pp. 168-181.

Right:
Black Lightning,
2012 (detail)
Glass, shoestrings,
found mop, bucket
and water
65 x 40 x 24 inches

ANATOMY

1. The Ovaries
Easter baskets,
matching egg cups of the flesh,
twin satellites of the moon.

Hot and cold faucets
turning on alternate months.

Maracas shaking their seeds
to the rhythm of blood.

A pair of bulbs
planted in body's earth
blooms to flowers
blossoming blood.

2. The Tubes

Perfect roads,
or snakes; ribbons
to tie into knots.

Jam up the tunnel,
hope it won't explode

3. The Womb

The warmest garment,
it grows like skin.

The most comfortable room,
it contains no furniture.

The easiest house,
 it builds itself.

The most generous country,
where the climate's always good.

Let the world go into its womb
again.
Turn out the lights, enjoy the
dark.

4. The Breasts

They are food
that likes to be eaten.

5. The Vagina

Tear this envelope open
gently for the letter inside
addressed to you,
that you'll read and reread
again and again,
until the red ink fades
into your hands,
until you know it in your veins.

Harryette Mullen

Previous:
Still Run Dry, 2012 (detail)
Glass, copper, rubber,
lead and steel
75 x 116 x 14 inches

Left:
Still Run Dry, 2012
Glass, copper, rubber,
lead and steel
75 x 116 x 14 inches

Right:
50 Proof, 2012
Glass, copper, rubber,
steel, soap, cotton
textiles, enamel basin
and water
63 x 27 x 20 inches

Left:
Mammy Machine, 2012
Glass, rubber, found chain
and washtub and water
75 x 36 x 24½ inches

Right:
Mammy Machine, 2012 (detail)

Left:
Black Lightning, 2012
Glass, shoestrings,
found mop, bucket
and water
65 x 40 x 24 inches

Right:
Weight, 2012
Fiberglass, wood, rope,
cotton scale, and
miscellaneous objects
80 x 65 x 24 inches

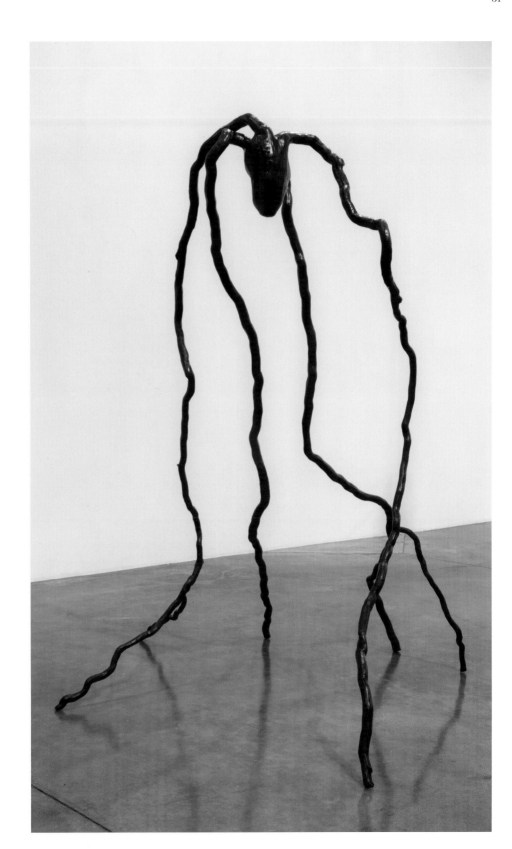

Previous:
Weight, 2012
Fiberglass, wood, rope,
cotton scale and
miscellaneous objects
80 x 65 x 24 inches

Left:
Hankerin' Heart: Hincty, 2012
Cast bronze
75 x 52 x 49 inches

Hankerin' Heart: Mosey, 2012
Cast bronze
66 x 49 x 59 inches

Hankerin' Heart: Gimpy, 2012
Cast bronze
64 x 61 x 53 inches

Right:
Hankerin' Heart: Gimpy, 2012

Left:
Undone, 2012
Fiberglass, cotton dress,
found chair and objects
198 x 72 x 60 inches

Right:
Undone, 2012 (detail)

Left:
Fall, 2011 (detail)
Photo: Tom Leeser

Right:
Fall, 2011
Cast bronze
159 x 42 x 39 inches

Left:
Rouse, 2012
Wood, bronze, paper and
antler sheds
90 x 76 x 73 inches

Right:
En Pointe, 2010
Wood, bronze,
graphite and rope
87 x 52 x 30 inches
Photo: Robert Wedemeyer
Courtesy LA Louver, Venice, CA

SHEDDING SKIN

Pulling out of the old scarred skin
(old rough thing I don't need now
I strip off
slip out of
leave behind)

I slough off deadscales
flick skinflakes to the ground

Shedding toughness
peeling layers down
to vulnerable stuff

And I'm blinking off old eyelids
for a new way of seeing

By the rock I rub against
I'm going to be tender again

Harryette Mullen

Harryette Mullen is the author of several poetry collections, including Recyclopedia: Trim-mings, *S*PeRM**K*T*, and *Muse & Drudge*, winner of a PEN Beyond Margins Award, and Sleeping with the Dictionary, a finalist for a National Book Award, National Book Critics Circle Award, and Los Angeles Times Book Prize. Her poems have been translated into Spanish, Portuguese, French, Italian, Polish, German, Swedish, Danish, Turkish, and Bul-garian. She teaches American poetry, African American literature, and creative writing at University of California, Los Angeles. A collection of her essays and interviews, *The Cracks Between What We Are and What We Are Supposed to Be*, is due from University of Alabama Press in 2012. Her *Tanka Diary* is forthcoming from Graywolf Press in 2013.

CHECKLIST

ALISON SAAR: STILL...

OTIS BEN MALTZ GALLERY
AUGUST 18 – NOVEMBER 17, 2012

All works by Alison Saar and courtesy of the artist and LA Louver, Venice, CA. Dimensions are in inches and height precedes width precedes depth. Single dagger (†) indicates work not traveling with the exhibition tour; double dagger (‡) indicates work added to the traveling portion of the exhibition.

En Pointe, 2010
Wood, bronze,
graphite and rope
87 x 52 x 30

Fall, 2011 †
Cast bronze
159 x 42 x 39

50 Proof, 2012
Glass, copper, rubber,
steel, soap, cotton textiles,
enamel basin and water
63 x 27 x 20

Black Lightning, 2012
Glass, shoestrings, found
mop, bucket and water
65 x 40 x 24

Hankerin' Heart: Gimpy, 2012
Cast bronze
64 x 61 x 53

Hankerin' Heart: Hincty, 2012
Cast bronze
75 x 52 x 49

Hankerin' Heart: Mosey, 2012
Cast bronze
66 x 49 x 59

Mammy Machine, 2012
Glass, rubber, found chain
and washtub and water
75 x 36 x 24 ½

Rouse, 2012
Wood, bronze, paper and
antler sheds
90 x 76 x 73

Still Run Dry, 2012
Glass, copper, rubber,
lead and steel
75 x 116 x 14

Undone, 2012 †
Fiberglass, cotton dress,
found chair and objects
198 x 72 x 60

Verstige, 2012 ‡
Fiberglass, wool, audio,
found trunk, suitcases
156 x 72 x 72

Weight, 2012
Fiberglass, wood, rope, cotton
scale and miscellaneous objects
80 x 65 x 24

ALISON SAAR: STILL...

Figge Art Museum
Davenport, IA
February 9—April 14, 2013

David C. Driskell Center
University of Maryland, College Park, MD
September 9—December 13, 2013

Sandra and David Bakalar Gallery
Massachusetts College of Art and Design, Boston, MA
January 22—March 8, 2014

Previous:
Rouse, 2012 (detail)

Right:
Vestige, 2012
Photo: Terri Baker
Courtesy Center for the
Living Arts, Mobile, AL

Photo: Tom Leeser

Alison Saar was born in Los Angeles and raised in the Laurel Canyon area.
She received her Bachelor of Art in studio art and art history in 1978 from
Scripps College, Claremont, California and her Master of Fine Art from Otis
Parsons Institute, now known as Otis College of Art and Design in Los Angeles
in 1981. Saar has held a number of distinguished artist residencies including
Studio Museum, New York, 1983; Roswell Museum of Art, New Mexico, 1985;
Washington Project for the Arts, Washington D.C., 1986; Hopkins Center,
Dartmouth College, New Hampshire, 2003. Saar has received two fellowships
from the National Endowment for the Arts in 1984 and 1988. She was awarded
the John Simon Guggenheim Memorial Foundation Fellowship in 1989, and the
Flintridge Foundation Award for Visual Artists in 2000.

Saar's work is included in numerous public collections, including the High
Museum, Atlanta, Georgia; Walker Institute, Minneapolis, Minnesota;
Museum of Fine Arts, Houston; Santa Barbara Museum of Art, Santa Barbara,
California; Virginia Museum of Fine Art, Richmond, Virginia; Hirshhorn
Museum and Sculpture Garden, Washington, D.C.; and in New York at the
Metropolitan Museum of Art, Museum of Modern Art and the Whitney
Museum of American Art where she was included in the 1993 Whitney Biennial.
She has done numerous public commissions including: "York" for Lewis and
Clark College; a Harriet Tubman Memorial "Swing Low" for the City of New
York; "Conjure" for the California Endowment in Los Angeles; "Califia" for
the Capital East End Complex in Sacramento; "Nocturne Navigator" for the
Columbus Ohio Museum of Art; "Monument to the Great Northern Migration"
in Bronxville, New York, MTA 125th St. Station. She lives and works in Los
Angeles and is represented by LA Louver in Venice, California.

Left:
Undone, 2012 (detail)
Fiberglass, cotton
dress, found chair
and objects
198 x 72 x 60 inches

THANK YOU!

Contemporary Collectors – Orange County
Art Alliance for Contemporary Glass – 50th Anniversary of Studio Glass Celebration

John Axtell
Ben Coombs
Kimberly Davis
Scott Darlington
Laura Daroca
Decker Studios
Amy Gantman
Parme Giuntini
Maddy, Kyle and Tom Leeser
Sarah Lewis
LA Louver
Sue Maberry
Harryette Mullen
John David O'Brien
Pilchuck Glass School
Margi Reeve
Angie Rodriguez
Anne Swett
Zane Tarver
Barbara Thompson
Sunny War
Chris Warner
OTIS Alumni Relations, Communications
Offices, Continuing Education, Facilities,
Liberal Arts and Science, Library,
Teaching Learning Center

Left:
Weight, 2012 (detail)
Fiberglass, wood, rope,
cotton scale, and
miscellaneous objects
80 x 65 x 24 inches

BEN MALTZ GALLERY

Meg Linton, Director of Galleries and Exhibitions
Jinger Heffner, Exhibition Coordinator and Gallery Registrar
Kathy MacPherson, Gallery Manager and Outreach Coordinator
Jeseca Dawson, 2012-2014 Curatorial Fellow
Alex Becerra, Preparator
Kirk Pickler, Preparator
John Weston, Preparator
Julia Marasa, Gallery Assistant
Rhonda Purdom, Gallery Assistant

OTIS Otis College of Art and Design

BEN MALTZ GALLERY

Otis College of Art and Design
Ben Maltz Gallery
9045 Lincoln Boulevard, Los Angeles, CA 90045
www.otis.edu/benmaltzgallery; galleryinfo@otis.edu; (310) 665-6905

©2012, **Alison Saar: STILL …**
Otis College of Art and Design, Ben Maltz Gallery
ISBN: 0-930209-33-8
SBN: 978-0-930209-33-9

Publisher: Otis College of Art and Design, Ben Maltz Gallery
Editor: Meg Linton
Designer: Anne Swett Predock
Design Assistant: Tina Miyakawa
Printer: V3
Edition: 1500
Photography: Unless noted otherwise, all photography by Chris Warner.

MIX
Paper from
responsible sources
FSC® C001755

ISBN: 978-0-930209-33-9